T0207754

A Plea For
Mercy
When Mercy Said No

MICHAEL ODAME-BOAHENE

WESTBOW
PRESS®
A DIVISION OF THOMAS NELSON
& ZONDERVAN

WestBow Press books may be ordered through booksellers or by contacting:

WestBow Press
A Division of Thomas Nelson & Zondervan
1663 Liberty Drive
Bloomington, IN 47403
www.westbowpress.com
1 (866) 928-1240

ISBN: 978-1-9736-2936-8 (sc)
ISBN: 978-1-9736-2935-1 (e)

Print information available on the last page.

WestBow Press rev. date: 05/29/2018

DEDICATION

To my mum, Ms Theresa Osae and my guardians, Ms Margaret Sakyiama and Mr. Benjamin Duodu; for the various ways you all contributed and supported to nurture me into the man I have become. Thank you for all you do. It is my heartfelt prayer that God will show you great mercies and everlasting kindness all the days of your life. Amen!

CONTENTS

CONTENTS

FOREWORD

It is a pleasure to introduce Minister Michael Odame-Boahene's, "A Plea for Mercy" to you. The content of this book came out from a man yearning to reach the heart of Jesus Christ. This book is thus an invitation to you to experience His Mercy, which has also been the heartbeat of God for all humanity. What you have in your own hands, as I have found myself, will be a blessing to you in three ways. First, it helps you to understand the concept of God's mercy and grace. Second, it unleashes the promise and the covenant of His mercy to man. Third, it opens one's mind on how to attract His mercy. Through this book, I have gained much understanding that, life is full of trespasses that put us against God. Such that attract divine judgement. God judgement has no appeal; more final than the Supreme Court's verdict. The only remedy there is, comes from Him too: His mercy reveals against His judgement. It is His mercy that prevails when we acknowledge the truth of our mess; when we cry for his compassion. It is prerogative that overlooks our mess and the punishment that we deserve. It makes us appear as though we never did it. We are justified-just as- if- we have never done it. This is the message of this book. In fact, the impact on my Spirit is compelling, after reading this book. It has given me the urge to recommend it to all. There is a well of compassion that flows through faith; a lake of mercy that abounds near the cross. Just call on the Lord to exercise it on your mess, the weight notwithstanding. He will grant you mercy, and this grace will give you blessings you don't deserve.

Dr. Alexander Adu Gyamfi
(The Presiding Bishop of Bible Believers' Tabernacle inc., New York)

ACKNOWLEDGEMENT

First and foremost, my heartfelt and eternal gratitude goes to the most merciful father who art in Heaven, my God in whom are hidden all the treasures of wisdom and knowledge, such as is required to produce a piece as this book. Glory to your Holy name.

My sincerest acknowledgement goes to my mother in the Lord, Prophetess Elizabeth Okrah Obeng (Founder of Jehovah Rapha Prayer Ministry), for all the support you give me in prayers alongside the spiritual guidance and instructions contributing to the craftmanship of this book.

I would also like to express my profound gratitude to my father in the Lord, Dr. Alexander Adu Gyamfi, the Presiding Bishop of Bible Believers' Tabernacle Inc., New York. Thank you for willingly providing the fore wording of this maiden piece and the various means by which you held my hand as a father to produce this book.

Again, I would like to express my thoughtful acknowledgement to Gloria Omari-Darteh, my confidant and editor-in-chief, whose prowess and intelligence was called to duty from the scratch to the production stages of this piece.

To my friend and sister Janet Konlan, founder and leader of the Gracious Youth Prayerline, for all your efforts and contributions in making this project a masterpiece.

Finally, I would like to acknowledge my friend Samuel Agbesi, my sister and brother Akosua Safoa Kesse and Kwaku Sefa Kesse respectively as well as all individuals and persons whose help in time went a long way to make this piece a success. God bless you all.

CHAPTER 1

THE CONCEPT OF GOD'S MERCY IN PERSPECTIVE

A wide array of vocabulary has been employed in order to achieve the goal of expressing the original language of God's mercy, with a wider collection of vocabulary being employed in the literal English translations. The nature of the various vocabularies used makes the concept more multifaceted and complicated to understand. Nevertheless, with the help of the Holy Ghost, we will make it work. The key to unlocking this mission to expound the concept of God's mercy is to look critically into the root words the various translators rendered as mercy in the Bible.

In the Bible, three fundamental root words express the concept of God's mercy in the Old Testament. Likewise, a group of three words expresses the concept of God's mercy in the New Testament. Let us explore!

Michael Odame-Boahene

1.1 MERCY IN THE OLD TESTAMENT

1. *Racham / rachamim:* The literal translation of this group of root words is "to show mercy, compassion, or pity". It has a close semblance to the root word rendered as womb. Thus makes it appropriate to be associated with the affection or compassion a mother has for her child as demonstrated by "...*the woman whose the living child was unto the king, for her bowels yearned upon her son, and she said, O my lord, give her the living child, and in no wise slay it. But the other said, Let it be neither mine nor thine, but divide it"* (1 Kings 3:26).

The kind of bond that exists between siblings as a result blood relationship can also be associated with this group of root words. Notice that a similar phrase "*bowels yearned*" that was rendered to demonstrate the affection of *the woman whose the living child was unto the king* for her child in the scripture above is also used to express Joseph's feelings for his brothers; "*And Joseph made haste; for his bowels did yearn upon his brother: and he sought where to weep; and he entered into his chamber, and wept there"* (Genesis 43:30).

In the same manner, God's mercy can be drawn in analogy to the various human relationships experienced in our society such as described below;

A mother's bond and affection toward a sucking child; "*Can a woman forget her sucking child, that she should not have compassion on the son of her womb? yea, they may forget, yet will I not forget thee"* (Isaiah 49:15).

A father's blood based bond to his children; "*Is Ephraim my dear son? is he a pleasant child? for since I spake against him, I do earnestly remember him still: therefore my bowels are troubled for him; I will surely have mercy upon him, saith the LORD"* (Jeremiah 31:20).

"Like as a father pitieth his children, so the LORD pitieth them that fear him" (Psalm 103:13)

[15] *"Look down from heaven, and behold from the habitation of thy holiness and of thy glory: where is thy zeal and thy strength, the sounding of thy bowels and of thy mercies toward me? are they restrained?* [16] *Doubtless thou art our father, though Abraham be ignorant of us, and Israel acknowledge us not: thou, O LORD, art our father, our redeemer; thy name is from everlasting"* (Isaiah 63:15-16).

A husband-wife relationship; [6] *"For the LORD hath called thee as a woman forsaken and grieved in spirit, and a wife of youth, when thou wast refused, saith thy God.* [7] *For a small moment have I forsaken thee; but with great mercies will I gather thee.* [8] *In a little wrath I hid my face from thee for a moment; but with everlasting kindness will I have mercy on thee, saith the LORD thy Redeemer"* (Isaiah 54:6-8).

2. *Chesed:* The King James Version will usually render this root word as mercy or kindness. Other versions as such as the NRSV, NAS, REB, NIV and the TEV translate it as "steadfast love" "lovingkindness", "loyalty" or "constant love", "love" or "unfailing love", "faithfulness" respectively. *Chesed* usually introduces an element of God's covenant of fidelity and permanence. It is often complimented with the characteristic of His goodness. The relation of God's covenant and His mercy (chesed) is explicit in the lines of *"And he said, LORD God of Israel, there is no God like thee, in heaven above, or on earth beneath, who keepest covenant and mercy with thy servants that walk before thee with all their heart"* (1 Kings 8:23).

"Know therefore that the LORD thy God, he is God, the faithful God, which keepeth covenant and mercy with them that love him and keep his commandments to a thousand generations" (Deut.7:9).

The element of permanence, expounded in God's chesed

have been demonstrated in phrases such as; "for the Lord is good, his mercy (chesed) is everlasting" or "his mercy endureth forever"; *"O give thanks unto the LORD; for he is good; for his mercy endureth for ever"* (1 Chronicles 16:34).

"O give thanks unto the LORD, for he is good: for his mercy endureth for ever" (Psalm 107:1).

Similarly, the translation of *racham* bears a close semblance to that of *chesed*. It can also be lined up in analogous series to the various levels of relationships and natural family experienced in our human society such as;

A husband-wife relationship; *"And it came to pass, when God caused me to wander from my father's house, that I said unto her, This is thy kindness which thou shalt shew unto me; at every place whither we shall come, say of me, He is my brother"* (Genesis 20:13),

A father-son relationship; *"And the time drew nigh that Israel must die: and he called his son Joseph, and said unto him, If now I have found grace in thy sight, put, I pray thee, thy hand under my thigh, and deal kindly and truly with me; bury me not, I pray thee, in Egypt"* (Genesis 47:29),

Host and guest as that of Rahab and the spies; *"Now therefore, I pray you, swear unto me by the LORD, since I have shewed you kindness, that ye will also shew kindness unto my father's house, and give me a true token"* (Joshua 2:12),

Friendship (David and Jonathan);[14] *"And thou shalt not only while yet I live shew me the kindness of the LORD, that I die not:* [15] *But also thou shalt not cut off thy kindness from my house for ever: no, not when the LORD hath cut off the enemies of David everyone from the face of the earth.* [16] *So Jonathan made a covenant with the house of David, saying, Let the LORD even require it at the hand of David's enemies.* [17] *And Jonathan caused David to swear again, because he loved him: for he loved him as he loved his own soul."* (1 Samuel 20:14-17).

3. *Chanan / chen:* Closely related to the character of grace or being gracious (Read more on the relationship between grace and mercy latter in chapter 2), this root word is translated to reflect the meaning of mercy and pity. The psalmist described one who is generous to the poor in the pharase *"... but the righteous sheweth mercy, and giveth"* (Psalm 37:21). Job said *"Have pity upon me, have pity upon me, O ye my friends; for the hand of God hath touched me"* (Job 19:21).

1.2 MERCY IN THE NEW TESTAMENT

1. *Splagchna:* Literally, Splagchna refers to the upper division of the human internal organs such as the heart, liver, lungs etc. This root word family has a close relation to the Hebrew *rachamim* and has the connotation of the sense of strong emotional feelings, especially compassion and affection. In most instances, Splagchna is translated to reflect Jesus' compassion for the blind, for a widow's plight, for a possessed child as well as the multitudes; *"But when he saw the multitudes, he was moved with compassion on them, because they fainted, and were scattered abroad, as sheep having no shepherd"* (Matthew 9:36).

2. *Eleos*: In the New Testament, this root word group has the largest collection of words translated as mercy. As far as Greek language is concerned, this word is often used to reflect a sign of weakness, the emotional extent of being overly lenient. Contrary to this, the New Testament does not share in this view, but rather shares in the assessment of the Old Testament perspective on God's mercy.

3. *Oiktirmos*: Oiktirmos is closely related to splagchna, and also rendered as "pity, mercy, compassion". It is mostly used together with splagchna. The relationship between oiktirmos and splagchna is revealed profoundly in the lines of the phrases "bowels of mercies" and "bowels and mercies" as expressed in *"Put on therefore, as the elect of God, holy and beloved, bowels of mercies, kindness, humbleness of mind, meekness, longsuffering;"* (Colossians 3:12) and

"If there be therefore any consolation in Christ, if any comfort of love, if any fellowship of the Spirit, if any bowels and mercies," (Philippians 2:1)

In summary, it is a known fact that in the quest to translate the mercy of God, both the Old Testament and the New Testament acknowledges the elements of God's grace, love, and faithfulness. They collectively form the make-up of the same material. The difference, however, is that the authors of the New Testament experienced God's mercy expressed in a much personified manner by Jesus Christ. He was the most potent manifestation of God's mercy, the ultimate assurance of that mercy for believers, and the source of their own mercy in their relationships with others. The message of a merciful, forgiving God was an integral part of the good news expressed by Jesus through His healings, miracles, fulfillment of His promises as well as the testimonies of others.

CHAPTER 2

THE MERCY AND GRACE NEXUS

In our discussion of God's mercy in the Old Testament in chapter 1, we mentioned that God's mercy has a connotation of an element of grace or being gracious, remember? Awesome. At this point, it is essential to draw the relationship between God's mercy and grace. The two terms are often confused and misconstrued. While they may have a close relation, it is vital to note that they are not the same.

Even in our arduous quest to live a righteous life to please the Lord, the prophet Isaiah reminds us that *"...all our righteousnesses are as filthy rags"* (Isaiah 64:6). As a matter of fact, the Bible categorically states that *"For all have sinned, and come short of the glory of God"* (Romans 3:23). *"For there is not a just man upon earth, that doeth good, and sinneth not"* (Ecclesiastes 7:20). As a result of that sin, we all deserve death; *"For the wages of sin is death; but the gift of God is eternal life through Jesus Christ our Lord"* (Romans 6:23). *"The soul that sinneth, it shall die. The son shall not bear the iniquity of the father, neither shall the father bear the iniquity of the son: the righteousness of the righteous shall be upon him, and the wickedness of the wicked shall be upon him"* (Ezekiel 18:20).

A plea for mercy is a desperate attempt that seeks to petition the merciful God to withhold the judgment we deserve, temper justice with mercy and instead grant to us the forgiveness we in no way have earned. God's response to our plea for His mercy in 1 John 1:9, *"...to forgive us our sins, and to cleanse us from all unrighteousness"* explains in short that mercy is God not giving us what we do deserve. In Habakkuk 3:2, the prophet asks the Lord to *"...in wrath remember mercy."* In Lamentations 3:22, the prophet Jeremiah confirms that *"It is of the LORD's mercies that we are not consumed, because his compassions fail not".* That is to say that, in the devil's attempt to hold our souls in ransom for the sins he incites us to commit against the Lord, God's mercy is the attribute that defends and rescues us. More explicitly, every day we live is an act of God's mercy. With this in mind, we can hitherto conclude that God's mercy is the very source of His people's life; *"[78]Through the tender mercy of our God; whereby the dayspring from on high hath visited us, [79]To give light to them that sit in darkness and in the shadow of death, to guide our feet into the way of peace"* (Luke 1:78-79). With this understanding, King David makes a desperate petition to God to *"Have mercy upon me, O God, according to thy lovingkindness: according unto the multitude of thy tender mercies blot out my transgressions"* (Psalm 51:1).

Whereas mercy is God not giving us what we do deserve, grace on the other hand is translated as God giving us something we do not deserve. After being pardoned and rescued from judgment by God's mercy, grace is anything and everything we receive beyond that mercy. Grace is simply defined as unmerited favor. We deserve nothing from God. God does not owe us anything. In light of this, anything good that we experience is as a result of the grace of God *"Every good gift and every perfect gift is from above, and cometh down from the Father of lights, with whom is no variableness, neither shadow of turning"* (James 1:17). God favors, or gives us good things that we do not deserve and could never earn.

A brighter picture of the relationship between these two variables (mercy and grace) was painted by Jesus' parable of the prodigal son in Luke 15:11-32. Let's take a moment to go through;

¹¹ And he said, A certain man had two sons: ¹² And the younger of them said to his father, Father, give me the portion of goods that falleth to me. And he divided unto them his living. ¹³And not many days after the younger son gathered all together, and took his journey into a far country, and there wasted his substance with riotous living. ¹⁴ And when he had spent all, there arose a mighty famine in that land; and he began to be in want. ¹⁵ And he went and joined himself to a citizen of that country; and he sent him into his fields to feed swine. ¹⁶ And he would fain have filled his belly with the husks that the swine did eat: and no man gave unto him. ¹⁷ And when he came to himself, he said, How many hired servants of my father's have bread enough and to spare, and I perish with hunger! ¹⁸ I will arise and go to my father, and will say unto him, Father, I have sinned against heaven, and before thee, ¹⁹ And am no more worthy to be called thy son: make me as one of thy hired servants. ²⁰ And he arose, and came to his father. But when he was yet a great way off, his father saw him, and had compassion, and ran, and fell on his neck, and kissed him. ²¹ And the son said unto him, Father, I have sinned against heaven, and in thy sight, and am no more worthy to be called thy son. ²² But the father said to his servants, Bring forth the best robe, and put it on him; and put a ring on his hand, and shoes on his feet: ²³ And bring hither the fatted calf, and kill it; and let us eat, and be merry: ²⁴ For this my son was dead, and is alive again; he was lost, and is found. And they began to be merry. ²⁵ Now his elder son was in the field: and as he came and drew nigh to the house, he heard musick and dancing.

²⁶ And he called one of the servants, and asked what these things meant. ²⁷ And he said unto him, Thy brother is come; and thy father hath killed the fatted calf, because he hath received him safe and sound. ²⁸ And he was angry, and would not go in: therefore came his father out, and intreated him. ²⁹ And he answering said to his father, Lo, these many years do I serve thee, neither transgressed I at any time thy commandment: and yet thou never gavest me a kid, that I might make merry with my friends: ³⁰ But as soon as this thy son was come, which hath devoured thy living with harlots, thou hast killed for him the fatted calf. ³¹ And he said unto him, Son, thou art ever with me, and all that I have is thine. ³² It was meet that we should make merry, and be glad: for this thy brother was dead, and is alive again; and was lost, and is found.

When the prodigal son returned to his father, the father demonstrated two character traits to him. First, he didn't give him what he deserved. The son knew he deserved some form of punitive measures. In fact, he acknowledged he deserved to lose his sonship and be counted among the servants. On the contrary, the father *had compassion* and withheld every form of punishment against him. At the expense of judgment and punishment, mercy said no. After that, he gave the son what he didn't deserve. *"The father said to his servants, Bring forth the best robe, and put it on him; and put a ring on his hand, and shoes on his feet".* Even his elder son who served his father *these many years* never experienced this kind of reward nor was he celebrated this way on any day. But the prodigal son had favor in the sight of his father and he was shown utmost grace at the expense of his elder brother who was more qualified than him.

The nexus of mercy and grace is best illustrated by the salvation that is available through Jesus Christ. We deserve judgment, but if we receive Jesus Christ as Savior, we receive mercy from God and judgment is withheld from us for His *"...mercy rejoiceth against judgment"* (James 2:13). Instead of judgment, we receive by grace salvation, forgiveness of sins, abundant life and an eternity in Heaven, the most wonderful place to spend eternity.

The author of Hebrews blends these two variables in one potent statement, admonishing, *"Let us therefore come boldly unto the throne of grace, that we may obtain mercy, and find grace to help in time of need* (Hebrews 4:16)." In this scripture, we are shown that our escape route to the destination of help during the time of trouble is via the intersection of mercy and grace. Without doing any critical analysis of grammar, it is essential to understand that in our quest to get to this destination, we first need to obtain mercy before finding grace. We can only obtain mercy after a desperate plea for mercy has been made to the merciful father who is the source of mercy. His response in granting this petition is the sure way to finding grace. At this point, help is released and supply replaces needs.

PRAYER CALL: Dear Lord, I acknowledge that you are the source of all mercy and grace. I pray that please grant me the ability to come boldly unto the throne of grace that I may obtain mercy and find grace to help in the time of need now and forever in the name of Jesus! Amen! Pray!

CHAPTER 3

GOD'S PREROGATIVE AND DESIRE FOR MERCY

When I was a kid in early Sunday school, I remember one of the songs we were taught literally translates "God is here, God is home, God is everywhere. When you sin, He'll see, hear, keep records of the sins and will never bless you". This song paints a rather gloomy picture of a faultfinding God, always looking for an opportunity to execute judgment against sinful humankind. It is rather unfortunate that the devil has succeeded in making people see a rather merciful God as captious, ever ready to keep records of our sins and execute judgment. Jesus did not come into the world to execute judgment. Nonetheless, the inevitable result of His coming is judgment because some refuse to believe and to make a plea for His mercy. *17For God sent not his Son into the world to condemn the world; but that the world through him might be saved.* *18He that believeth on him is not condemned: but he that believeth not is condemned already, because he hath not believed in the name of the only begotten Son of God.* (John 3:17-18). This is neither a move to flag a campaign for the perpetuation of evil and sinful acts nor a vote for the promotion of unrighteousness but to express in clear succinct terms that if God was to bless us for our righteousness, I don't know how many people would qualify, having established that *"all our righteousnesses are as filthy rags"*

Registered at the heart of God's exclusive plan for salvation after the fall of man, is a blueprint of God's desire for mercy i.e. the exercise of the prerogative of mercy and granting of pardon by withholding judgment. In Hosea 6:6, the prophet profoundly expresses God's desire for mercy in the words *"...I desired mercy..."* A proficient exposition of this was revealed by Jesus in two analogies. First, He tasks the Pharisees to learn what God meant by promulgating *"I desire mercy"* when they complained to His disciples *"Why eateth your Master with publicans and sinners?"* Jesus knowing they will never understand, He advances to explain this further that *"...I am not come to call the righteous, but sinners to repentance"* (Matthew 9:10-13). God's desire for mercy rings a call to repentance, which eventually translates into a call to life and for that matter, successful life. It is only God's desire for mercy that will let Him disregard man's fallible nature and use him to accomplish His own purpose. The exercise of God's prerogative of mercy does not take into account the gravity of one's sins. God's mercies are potent enough to turn every mess into a message and every state of ridicule into a miracle.

In the second analogy, Jesus justifies the acts of His disciples even by likening them to David when they *"...were an hungred, and began to pluck the ears of corn and to eat."* [2] *But when the Pharisees saw it, they said unto him, Behold, thy disciples do that which is not lawful to do upon the sabbath day. ³But he said unto them, Have ye not read what David did, when he was an hungred, and they that were with him; ⁴How he entered into the house of God, and did eat the shewbread, which was not lawful for him to eat, neither for them which were with him, but only for the priests? ⁵Or have ye not read in the law, how that on the sabbath days the priests in the temple profane the sabbath, and are blameless? ⁶But I say unto you, that in this place is one greater than the temple. ⁷But if ye had known what this meaneth, I will have mercy, and not sacrifice, ye would not have condemned the guiltless* (Matthew 12:1-7). God's mercy grants immunity from the accusations of the devil and also grants impunity from further unwarranted attacks of the devil, even when your actions or inactions call for such attacks. When we are confronted by and limited to laws, rules and principles (natural or supernatural), God's mercy acts as an advocacy to defy those odds. It disregards human flaws and grants satisfaction to human quest. You may by one reason or the other gotten yourself into a condition you could have avoided by virtue of hunger or a burning desire as in the case of David and the priests; it is time to make a Plea for Mercy! In this wise, you are making an acknowledgement of God's mercy as the factor that can cause a stir in your situation and bring you to an expected end. In other words, when you miss your route in life, a plea for God's mercy is an assured aid to redirect your path into your destiny. As you read through the pages of this book, it is my heartfelt prayer that God will have mercy on you, cause a stir in your situation and bring you to an expected end. May God usher your path into your destiny at this hour in the name of Jesus! Amen!

It is cardinal to note that God's desire for mercy expounds His characteristic nature of care for the needs of mankind.

God's mercy is never just a feeling but symbolic of His will and expressed by His actions. His desire for mercy stands as a vote of His commitment to provide for you, protect you, deliver you, proclaim liberty for you, open doors for you, heal you etc. In effect, it is a blessed assurance not just to make you survive, but also to thrive in this adulterous and sinful generation.

As a sovereign God, His desire for mercy stands in defense of His choices. The Apostle Paul expounds this in Romans 9:11-16; *[11](For the children being not yet born, neither having done any good or evil, that the purpose of God according to election might stand, not of works, but of him that calleth;). [12]It was said unto her, The elder shall serve the younger. [13]As it is written, Jacob have I loved, but Esau have I hated. What shall we say then? [14]Is there unrighteousness with God? God forbid. [15]For he saith to Moses, I will have mercy on whom I will have mercy, and I will have compassion on whom I will have compassion. [16]So then it is not of him that willeth, nor of him that runneth, but of God that sheweth mercy.* When God speaks, acts or makes a choice, no one can question the rationale behind His option. However, the Apostle Paul gives us a hint that what informs God's decision is desire for mercy. Can you imagine how your life would be if you obtained mercy at any point? It places you on God's radar of priorities and makes you His inevitable option. At this point, I dare to infer that on the account of man's desire to succeed, an element of God's mercy is inevitable. It is therefore incumbent upon us in all our endeavors to make a plea for mercy!

PRAYER CALL: Merciful father, I thank you for my life. I pray that from today let the proceeds of my life hang on your mercy in the name of Jesus. Amen!

CHAPTER 4

THE MERCY SEAT

¹⁷ *And thou shalt make a mercy seat of pure gold: two cubits and a half shall be the length thereof, and a cubit and a half the breadth thereof. ¹⁸ And thou shalt make two cherubims of gold, of beaten work shalt thou make them, in the two ends of the mercy seat. ¹⁹ And make one cherub on the one end, and the other cherub on the other end: even of the mercy seat shall ye make the cherubims on the two ends thereof. ²⁰ And the cherubims shall stretch forth their wings on high, covering the mercy seat with their wings, and their faces shall look one to another; toward the mercy seat shall the faces of the cherubims be. ²¹ And thou shalt put the mercy seat above upon the ark; and in the ark thou shalt put the testimony that I shall give thee. ²² And there I will meet with thee, and I will commune with thee from above the mercy seat, from between the two cherubims which are upon the ark of the testimony, of all things which I will give thee in commandment unto the children of Israel* (Exodus 25:17-22).

The Ark of the Covenant was made to simulate a token that represented the presence of God. In fulfillment of His promise of taking them to the Promised Land, His presence amongst them was inevitable. However, God said to Moses; "...*I will not go up in the midst of thee; for thou art a stiffnecked people: lest I consume thee in the way...*" (Exodus 33:3). In order for God to dwell among them without consuming them, there was the need for Him to develop a buffer system that would prevent this problem; a system that would withhold His judgment against them whenever they disobey Him and go their own way. God's mercy serves as the paramount potent characteristic that could be simulated as a buffer system against judgment. Out of the infinite characteristic attributes of God, His mercy is the only attribute that is registered on the Ark of the Covenant of God. In unequivocal terms, the idea behind the development and the building of the Ark was as an act of God's mercy. The mercy seat was designed to be the cover/lid of the ark, signifying that God's presence was always covered in the characteristic of His mercy. This act was necessary to avert the prospective reaction of consuming them.

In perspective, when you take a closer look at the Ark from any angle of inclination, the mercy seat will still be visible. Essentially, God's mercy is available for everyone just to carry you through regardless your religious lenses and belief systems. A *Plea for Mercy* is all you need to make. One thing the cover or lid of a container does is that it prevents externalities from influencing or contaminating the content of the container. The cover of God's mercy prevents us from being devoured by the devil. When the devil launches any attack from the pit of hell against you, mercy says no.

4.1 THE ROLE OF THE MERCY SEAT

After God had instructed them on the dimensions and specifications of the Ark, He concluded by specifying the role the mercy seat will serve. He said *I will meet with thee, and I will commune with thee from above the mercy seat...* This statement reveals the two main purposes the mercy seat was designed to serve;

1. *Rendezvous* – A "casual" meeting place sort of, where God always had an appointment with His people. If there was any place they could be 100% sure of meeting God, it was at the place of the mercy seat. If there is a place where divinity fulfills an appointment with humanity, it is at the place of the mercy seat. One of the significant things that happen when humanity encounters divinity is the grant of pardon and withholding of judgement. Yes, this is the only place where a sinful person can petition a righteous judge and receive pardon. The mercy seat is the place where God decides to overlook the frailties and fallibilities of man and show forth his capabilities. This is the point where God's *"...strength is made perfect in weakness"* (2 Corinthians 12:9). This accounts for the enormous victories, breakthroughs, miracles, signs and wonders they encountered any time they carried along the Ark.

   In analogy, let us consider this scripture: *[14] when the people removed from their tents, to pass over Jordan, and the priests bearing the ark of the covenant before the people; [15] And as they that bare the ark were come unto Jordan, and the feet of the priests that bare the ark were dipped in the brim of the water,*

(for Jordan overfloweth all his banks all the time of harvest,)
[16] That the waters which came down from above stood and rose
up upon an heap very far from the city Adam, that is beside
Zaretan: and those that came down toward the sea of the plain,
even the salt sea, failed, and were cut off: and the people passed
over right against Jericho. [17] And the priests that bare the ark of
the covenant of the LORD stood firm on dry ground in the midst
of Jordan, and all the Israelites passed over on dry ground,
until all the people were passed clean over Jordan (Joshua
3:14-17). Notice the readiness of the waters (overflowing
its banks at that time) to stand still and make way at the
point of contact with the Ark of the Covenant. Water in
scripture is sometimes used to connote God's judgement.
The moment mercy showed up, judgment (the waters)
made way. The water that stood still here demonstrates
the readiness of God to withhold judgement and make
a way where there seems to be no way. This is significant
because at the mercy seat, *"...mercy rejoiceth against*
judgment" (James 2:13).

The mercy seat served as the platform that "trapped"
the presence of God and His Glory among His people,
the official seat of the Lord of Host among His people.
It became a symbol and token of His divine presence.
Paul teaches that *"...your body is the temple of the Holy*
Ghost which is in you" (1 Corinthians 6:19). Thus God has
fashioned you as an individual as a potential carrier of
His divine presence just as the Ark. What is required
here is a system that positions you at a vantage point
where you can "trap" His divine presence: a system that
makes it possible for humanity to carry divinity at any

point in time regardless their imperfection. That system is called the mercy seat and it can simply be instituted by making a desperate plea for mercy. This platform also becomes a divine covering that God establishes over you.

2. *Communications Protocol* – The mercy seat was modelled to serve as a system that allows information to be disseminated between God and His people. This was the system that generated God's commandments and directions to His people as captured in the phrase *"of all things which I will give thee in commandment unto the children of Israel"* (Exodus 25:22). God's directions for the children of Israel were encrypted via the mercy seat. Thus without the mercy seat, it was almost impossible for God to direct them. In our routine communication with God, it is critical to engage the mercy seat in order to attract God's directions for our lives. When you are lost and in need of directions, the most viable option would be to run to the mercy seat. That is the only system that can assuredly lead you to your destination.

PRAYER CALL: Dear Lord, thank you for reminding me that I am still a potential carrier of your divine presence despite my human frailties and imperfections. I petition you at the mercy seat to reposition me at vantage point to trap your presence all the days of my life. Also, please cover my loved (mention names) ones and me in your mercies all the days of our lives in the name merciful name of Jesus! Amen!

CHAPTER 5

THE PROMISE AND COVENANT OF MERCY

This chapter does not seek to discuss the subject matter of covenant versus its pros and cons but I don't know how the exploit of this theme (mercy) would have been completed without introducing the aspect of covenant. In essence, the effect of God's mercy is sealed when it is captured under the umbrella of covenant. When mercy is underpinned by covenant, salvation is assured. That presupposes that any activity performed under the covenant of mercy produces assured and expected results. Covenanting with God on His mercy is therefore an inevitable act as far as the christian living is concerned.

Consider this scripture; *7For a small moment have I forsaken thee; but with great mercies will I gather thee. 8 In a little wrath I hid my face from thee for a moment; but with everlasting kindness will I have mercy on thee, saith the LORD thy Redeemer. 9For this is as the waters of*

Noah unto me: for as I have sworn that the waters of Noah should no more go over the earth; so have I sworn that I would not be wroth with thee, nor rebuke thee (Isaiah 54:7-9).

Wait a minute! Did you realize the turn of events here? God makes a U-turn from His justifiable wrath to promise mercy? Normally, the first and ideal course of action of a person who has been offended so bad consistently by the same person or a group of persons would most likely be a loss of tolerance and subsequently react in a manner that would let him express his wrath, most probably through judgement or punishment if applicable. This is especially true about leadership. Is it not ironic that He promises to show mercy instead of towing the path of passing judgement and punishment?

Get this right, God is not delighted in forsaking you nor leaving you to the enemy to scatter you even in your worst state of sin. Remember *while we were yet sinners, Christ died for us* just to waive the judgement and punishment we deserved. His interest to *gather thee* back from the grips of the enemy is demonstrated in His emphasis on showing you mercy and for that matter, *great mercies.* God also demonstrate an act of making up for that *small moment* of forsaking you by the promise of mercy *with everlasting kindness.* In His bid to promise mercy, He also reveals that the only attribute that can replace His wrath is His mercy. Now, that is an admission that the magnitude of His mercies is greater than His wrath. Hallelujah! The expression of this promise explains that His everlasting mercy stand as the antidote to His temporary wrath.

Backtracking to the previous chapter (chapter 4), you will recall we mentioned that water in scripture is sometimes used to connote the judgement of God during our discussion on the mercy seat. Fast-forward to our current discussion, you will realize that in the verse 9 of Isaiah 54, God introduces the simile of withholding back the *waters of Noah* to His wrath. He underpins this by introducing the element of swearing to an oath in the lines of "*I have sworn*". The element of covenant can be identified in the expression of swearing to an oath. Just as He has sworn to withhold judgement (the *waters of Noah),* so has He sworn to withhold His wrath. The net effect is an assurance of covenanting to show mercy.

In the exercise of showing mercy, God did not choose to bind Himself to a covenant for the sake of expression of interest. It is an invitation to mankind to take advantage of the conditions of a covenant and be a beneficiary of the full compliments of the His comprehensive redemption plan embedded in the covenant. The unequivocal expression of this intent is an indication that God has already committed to appending His signature on this deal because "*God is not a man, that He should lie, nor a son of man, that He should repent. Has He said, and will He not do? Or has He spoken, and will He not make it good?* (Numbers 23:19). Now, God Himself has sent out the invitation to you to partake in this covenant. It is your sole responsibility and duty to accept by making a plea for mercy.

5.1 THE SURE MERCIES OF DAVID

So many monumental things and events have been recorded in the bible about David. Apparently, David is the second most talked about character in the Old Testament. Almost every kid who has ever attended Sunday school knows about the famous story of David and Goliath. David has been described as the young shepherd boy who killed the giant Goliath with a simple one stone slingshot without sweat. It is common knowledge that this brave young shepherd boy has gone down history to register his name as one of Israel's greatest kings. We know that Jesus Christ is a descendant of the house of king David. Just to mention a few, did David achieve all these feats by fluke? Certainly, not and that is what this topic seeks to unravel.

One would easily presume the above description to fit a perfect man running a perfect life as in the case of Job whom God Himself testified about as "*a perfect and an upright man*". Was that the case of David? Certainly not. In fact, David himself testified of what said about him in 1 Chronicles 28:3; "*But God said unto me, Thou shall not build an house for my name, because thou has been a man of war, and hast shed blood*". God never testified of David as "*a perfect and an upright man*" but guess what, God described him as a "*man after mine own heart*" (Acts 13:22). One would have thought that God would rather make "*a perfect and an upright man*" a "*man after mine own heart*" and not otherwise, considering the fact He is a holy and an upright God himself.

David had a covenant with God which was not peculiar to him alone because most of the men who attained great heights and feats in scriptures also had a covenant with God. What made David's covenant with God outstanding amongst the others was the fact that it was underpinned by the mercy of God. The difference was spelled out clearly by the mercy of God.

Now, consider this scripture; "*Incline your ear, and come to Me. Hear, and your soul shall live; And I will make an everlasting covenant with you, even the sure mercies of David*" (Isaiah 55:3). The expression "*the sure mercies of David*" makes an impeccable description of the kind of covenant God had with David.

In succinct terms, this kind of covenant could never fail under any given circumstance beyond human capacity and comprehension. Yes, God never breaks His covenant because He is a faithful God but man is liable to do so. If any covenant between God and a man failed, it is simply because man could not hold on to honor his commitment of the covenant. However, with this kind of covenant God made with David, it was impossible for it to fail because it was underpinned by the mercy of God. Anytime David in his own human frailties breached any of the terms and conditions of the covenant, God's mercy acted as a buffer system to adjust these terms and conditions and keep it running.

God, in this scripture extends an invitation to man to have a taste of the *sure mercies of David*. The key factor that is required of you to establish this covenant is your ability to hear His voice. However, this scripture prompts us that you cannot live within any locality and expect to hear God's voice. There is a certain angle of inclination within which you can attain that frequency modulation of hearing His voice and it is always important to locate yourself within that catchment area because it enhances your chances of hearing His voice crystal clear. Your tendency to survive depends on your ability to hear and obey God's voice.

God doesn't just desire to make a regular covenant with you but the one that is up to the standards of the *sure mercies of David*. Hearing God is critical a factor here because it is easier to obey God when you can hear His voice. That notwithstanding, in this kind of covenant, even if you fail to honor your commitment to the terms and conditions because of your inexplicable human frailties, you are still covered by his mercies.

Michael Odame-Boahene

PRAYER CALL: Oh Lord, my father, I pray that at this hour with everlasting kindness, show me great mercies and remember me according to your word. I pray again that establish your covenant with me, even the sure mercies of David in the most powerful name of Jesus! Amen!

CHAPTER 6

ATTRACTING GOD'S MERCY

J esus, while he walked in the shoes of His father on the earth, saw the need to promulgate the proven system of attracting God's mercy. In this system, He teaches that *Blessed are the merciful: for they shall obtain mercy* (Matthew 5:7). The principle here is that mercy begets mercy. In other words, showing mercy serves as a bait to hold on to God's mercy. Again, in the Lord's prayer, Jesus teaches us to pray to God to "*forgive us our debts, as we forgive our debtors*" (Matthew 6:12). By inference, Jesus was teaching us that it is only by showing mercy towards other people that we can obtain the moral right to plea for God's mercy. The only commanding sequence that God's mercy responds to is expressing mercy to other people.

In this teaching, Jesus also underscores one very critical factor that comes by expressing mercy; He calls the merciful, *blessed.* Every blessing you can think of that comes with living a victorious Christian life can be associated with the virtue of mercy. Living as a vessel of dispensing mercy to others is a way of depositing into your account of blessing. When counting your blessing, don't skip your gestures of showing mercy, for it is a blessing to be merciful. If we take a critical look at the reverse of this scripture, it would read "cursed are the unmerciful; for they shall not obtain mercy". Neglecting the responsibility of expressing mercy to other people is a process of engineering a self-destructive tool that has the propensity of inflicting undesired wounds on oneself.

Jesus gave a hypothetical analogy of this proven system of attracting God's mercy using the parable of the good Samaritan in Luke 10:30-37;

30 And Jesus answering said, A certain man went down from Jerusalem to Jericho, and fell among thieves, which stripped him of his raiment, and wounded him, and departed, leaving him half dead. 31 And by chance there came down a certain priest that way: and when he saw him, he passed by on the other side. 32 And likewise a Levite, when he was at the place, came and looked on him, and passed by on the other side. 33 But a certain Samaritan, as he journeyed, came where he was: and when he saw him, he had compassion on him, 34 And went to him, and bound up his wounds, pouring in oil and wine, and set him on his own beast, and brought him to an inn, and took care of him. 35 And on the morrow when he departed, he took out two pence, and gave them to the host, and said unto him, Take care of him; and whatsoever thou spendest more, when I come again, I will repay thee. 36 Which now of these three, thinkest thou, was neighbour unto him that fell among the thieves? 37 And he said, He that shewed mercy on him. Then said Jesus unto him, Go, and do thou likewise.

In this parable, Jesus issues a very remarkable order. He says, "*Go, and do thou likewise*". In other words, go and show mercy to your neighbor as the Samaritan did. For the avoidance of doubt, Jesus clearly describes who a neighbor is. The parable plots that "*a certain man went down from Jerusalem to Jericho*". I bet this man was a Jew and thus reviled by the Samaritans. He probably might be a kinsman of the priest and the Levite. However, that did not answer to the question of who a neighbor is. The perfect answer was "*He that shewed mercy on him.*" The lesson here is that you don't only have to extend the arm of mercy to people you are closely related to (family and friends) but to non-relatives, even people who have insatiable disaffection and hatred for you.

A critical appreciation of this parable clearly reveals God's direction for His people in terms of cohabiting with one another. God expects His people to come alive in the courts of mercy. He prefers a people who show feelings of affinity toward Him and extend the arm of mercy toward each other to a people who go about the discharge of their religious duty in a perfunctory manner or merely formal way.

The priest and the levite are symbolic of sacrifice. They were both busily going about their religious duty of rendering sacrifice but no matter how they aced the discharge of their responsibilities, it was irrelevant at this point. Many are caught in the engagement of religious trifles in the name of practicing extreme religious formalisms. Don't get me wrong, I'm not passing judgement against you. I believe it is good to offer sacrifices but sacrificing at the expense of showing mercy amounts to an act of futility. Every sacrifice is made perfect on the altar of mercy.

It is amazing how we keep money in our savings accounts with the motive of salvaging the occurrence of an emergency and yet pray to God for divine protection whereas there are victims of various levels of hopeless situations starving of a kind gesture to aid them survive. A spectacular example is a visit to the sick at the hospital who cannot even afford their medical bills but in our hypocrisy, we tend to have the effrontery to pray to God to heal them when we know that all they need is money and not prayer. The greatest tool the enemy uses to obstruct the expression of mercy is the preoccupation with trifles in life. The tyranny of triviality will always result in the curse of the unmerciful.

PRAYER CALL: Merciful father, thank you for exposing me to your word. I pray that rid me of the preoccupation with religious trifles in life. In the name of Jesus, I pray that help me to show mercy that I may also obtain your mercy. Amen!

CHAPTER 7

GOD'S SHEEPDOGS (GOODNESS AND MERCY)

Almost every church has adopted a common practice that at the end of the service we all join in the chorus of making that confession, "*Surely goodness and mercy shall follow me all the days of my life: and I will dwell in the house of the* LORD *forever*" (Psalm 23:6). I'm yet to come across a believer who is not familiar with this scripture or at least hasn't heard it at all. I am tempted to think that we have been so used to this structure of closing church service that our attitude does not reflect the confession we make. Wait a minute! Before you start throwing jabs at me, let me state categorically that I am not against making this confession. I believe so much in that prayer and I am for it. However, I shudder to think that it is more or less losing its focus to the adoption as a "church mantra" for dispersing the assembly of the believers. This chapter will attempt to cast a shade of light on this confession.

It is very fascinating how God demonstrates the nexus of His goodness and mercy towards us. Throughout scripture, God has demonstrated His goodness in a manner that is tied to the dispensation of His mercies. This has been experienced both in the past and present age. The psalmist advocates; *"O give thanks unto the LORD; for he is good: for his mercy endures forever"* (Psalm 136:1). The above scripture and many others alike expose how God's goodness and mercy compliments each other.

Let's take a look at this scripture in Romans 2:4; *"Or do you despise the riches of His goodness, forbearance, and longsuffering, not knowing that the goodness of God leads you to repentance?"* this scripture throws more light on the interconnectivity of God's goodness and mercy. At this point, we can all agree that repentance is a product of God's mercy. In this light, it is equitable to conclude that the objective of this scripture is to reveal how God's goodness is connected to His mercy. In other words, it is nearly impossible to enjoy God's goodness without experiencing a fair share of His mercy.

A clear line of this argument can be drawn from the account of scripture, which states, *"There was a man in the land of Uz, whose name was Job; and that man was blameless and upright, and one who feared God and shunned evil. ² And seven sons and three daughters were born to him. ³ Also, his possessions were seven thousand sheep, three thousand camels, five hundred yoke of oxen, five hundred female donkeys, and a very large household, so that this man was the greatest of all the people of the East. ⁴ And his sons would go and feast in their houses, each on his appointed day, and would send and invite their three sisters to eat and drink with them. ⁵ So it was, when the days of feasting had run their course, that Job would send and sanctify them, and he would rise early in the morning and offer burnt offerings according to the number of them all. For Job said, "It may be that my sons have sinned and cursed God in their hearts." Thus Job did regularly"* (Job 1:1-5).

The above scripture informs us of how God showed His goodness towards Job by blessing him on every side and area of life with possessions in both subjects and objects. In fact, the scripture states categorically that *this man was the greatest of all the people of the East.* Despite all his possessions, which even transcended to the glamor his sons enjoyed, he understood how critical it is to compliment the goodness of God with His mercy. Having this knowledge, Job developed the attitude of making a desperate plea for mercy to cover his sons. *So it was, when the days of feasting had run their course, that Job would send and sanctify them, and he would rise early in the morning and offer burnt offerings according to the number of them all. For Job said, "It may be that my sons have sinned and cursed God in their hearts." Thus Job did regularly".* He assumed they might ignore the one most important thing that they needed to compliment and complete all the luxury they possessed so he took a proactive step to right that wrong.

7.1 PLAYING WITH THE SHEEPDOGS

As the good shepherd as He is, goodness and mercy are God's choicest tools engineered to guard His herd sheep. These are what I appropriately describe as "sheepdogs". By way of introduction, sheepdogs are dogs trained to guard and herd sheep. In general, the sheep do not like the sheepdogs because the later has the semblance of a wolf. The difference between the sheepdog and the wolf is that the sheepdog dares not and cannot attack the sheep. The sheepdog understands that in order to guard the sheep to safety, violence is sometimes an option. Despite the fact that the sheep prefers to go along their merry way oblivious to the perils of life, it is the duty of the sheep to devise a means of accommodating and tolerating the presence of the sheepdog in order to keep the wolves away. In the event of an attack, the entire herd sheep manage to desperately take cover under the shadow of the sheepdogs.

Likewise, God has trained His sheepdogs in the attributes of His Goodness and mercy to guard us (His sheep) throughout the journey to our destination. Jesus issues a word of caution to us that *"Behold, I send you out as sheep in the midst of wolves..."* (Matthew 10:16). Wolves are usually malicious. They are the exact contrast of the sheep. Whereas the sheep are usually quiet and peace loving, wolves are chaotic and violent in nature. They possess evil characteristics. But anytime the wolves of life in the form of diseases, depression, disappointments, pain, scandals, principalities, powers etc. attack, we can run to take cover in the guarding prowess of God's sheepdogs which guarantees safety to our destination.

Our duty is to recognize the presence of these sheepdogs in our daily routine and make sure we accommodate them just so we do not end up driving them away. Their absence in our lives amounts to an open invitation to these wolves to unnecessarily attack and devour us. It is important to note that these two sheepdogs work together as a team. However, it is easy to recognize and accommodate one than the other. We all enjoy the goodness of God both in attribute and in the form of blessings He showers on us. The difficulty here is that we fail to recognize and plea for mercy which is the compliment and teammate of God's goodness, working together as sheepdogs. The quality of life enjoyed is a function of the mutual symbiosis existing between the characteristics of God's goodness and mercy. In order to harness the ultimate potential of these sheepdogs, it is critical to allow them function together as a team. It is very critical for us not to ignore this key player called mercy. I urge you to make a desperate plea for mercy now.

David had a penchant for these sheepdogs. His open confession that "*Surely goodness and mercy shall follow me all the days of my life: and I will dwell in the house of the LORD forever*" was an invitation to the sheepdogs to guard and protect him, trusting in their expertise to keep him safe and sound in the midst of the fiery wolves. He understood they would gladly pursue him once he invited them. To get the complete understanding of this concept, it is essential to note that the english rendition "follow" does not really reflect the true meaning of the original Hebrew word (*rādaph*), which *also* means "to pursue, chase, and attend closely upon." In perspective of the original word, the sheepdogs' assignment is to jealously guard and protect the sheep until safety, soundness and peace is achieved in the midst of the wolves.

PRAYER CALL: Merciful father, thank you for exposing me to your sheepdogs of goodness and mercy. I pray that help me not to ignore any of the teammates. As you release unto me these sheepdogs, I pray that grant me the ability to accommodate them as they guard and protect me to my destination in the midst of the wolves to secure my safety and soundness even in the powerful name of Jesus. AMEN! Pray now!

Now I declare that surely goodness and mercy shall follow me all the days of my life: and I will dwell in the house of the LORD forever, AMEN!

Printed in the United States
By Bookmasters